Kent —
a little sex
comedy for a
sexy guy!

Heat Wave

XXX

Bill

HEAT WAVE

BY MICHEL MARC BOUCHARD
TRANSLATED BY BILL GLASSCO

Heat Wave
first published 1996 by
Scirocco Drama
An imprint of J. Gordon Shillingford Publishing Inc.
© Michel Marc Bouchard, 1991
English Translation © Bill Glassco, 1995
Originally published in French as
Les grandes chaleurs, Leméac Editeur, 1993

Cover design by Terry Gallagher/Doowah Design
Author's photo by Robert Laliberté
Translator's photo by Michel Boulianne
Printed and bound in Canada by Les Ateliers Graphiques Marc Veilleux

Published with the generous assistance of The Canada Council.

Canadian Cataloguing in Publication Data

Bouchard, Michel Marc, 1958-
[Grandes chaleurs. English]
Heat wave

A Play.
Translation of: Les grandes chaleurs.
ISBN 1-896239-09-9

I. Glassco, Bill II. Title: Grandes chaleurs. English.

PS8553.O7745G7213 1996   C842'.54   C96-900008-1
PR9199.3.B61G7213 1996

...to my mother's jokes and my father's laughter

Characters

GISÈLE Cloutier: A woman in her fifties, recently widowed. The mother of twins, she's been having an affair with YANNICK the past two months.

YANNICK: A young man of twenty, recently a delinquent.

NAPOLÉON Bonneau: A man in his fifties. Has the neighbouring cottage to the Cloutiers. An incorrigible handyman, he's had his eye on GISÈLE for years.

LOUISETTE: Thirty. GISÈLE's daughter and twin to LOUIS.

LOUIS: Thirty. GISÈLE's son and twin to LOUISETTE.

Setting

A beach. A summer cottage. July.

Production History

Les grandes chaleurs premiered in August, 1991, at the Théâtre de la Fenière in Ancienne-Lorette (Quebec City) under the artistic direction of Marielle Kirouac. It was directed by Jacques Lessard and performed by Marielle Kerouac (GISÈLE), Carol Casistat (YANNICK), Jacques-Henri Gagnon (NAPOLÉON), Simone Chartrand (LOUISETTE), and Réjean Vallée (LOUIS).

Heat Wave premiered in August, 1995, at Theatre Lac Brome in Knowlton, Quebec, under the artistic direction of Nicholas Pynes with the following cast:

GISÈLE .... Joanna Noyes
YANNICK .... Keath Thome
NAPOLÉON .... George Sperdakos
LOUISETTE .... Cary Lawrence
LOUIS .... Marcel Jeannin

Directed by Bill Glassco
Set and costumes designed by Jennifer Cook
Lighting designed by Luc Prairie
Stage Manager: Kathryn Cleveland

Michel Marc Bouchard

Born in 1958 in Lac St. Jean, Quebec, Michel Marc Bouchard holds a B.A. in Theatre from the University of Ottawa, and has worked as an actor, director and teacher. His seven published plays include the highly acclaimed *Les Feluettes* (*Lilies*), 1987; *Les Muses Orphelines* (*The Orphan Muses*), 1989, and *L'Histoire de l'oie* (*The Tale of Tikka*), 1991. Since Heat Wave, he has written two other comedies set around Lac aux Sangsues (Leech Lake), *Les Papillons de nuit* (1992) and *Le Désir* (1995), which, like their predecessor, have been frequently produced in summer theatres across Quebec. His plays have been translated into English, Italian, Spanish, German, Dutch and Bulgarian, and performed extensively in Europe. For *Lilies* (translated by Linda Gaboriau) he was the 1991 recipient of both the Dora Mavor Moore and Floyd S. Chalmers Awards, and has been a three time finalist for the Governor General's Literary Award. His most recent play, *Le Voyage du couronnement*, premiered in September, 1995 at Montreal's Théâtre du Nouveau Monde.

Bill Glassco

Bill Glassco is the founding artistic director of Toronto's Tarragon Theatre, co-founding artistic director of the Canadian Stage Company, and one of this country's best known directors of Canadian work. With John van Burek he translated seven plays of Michel Tremblay, and, on his own, Simon Fortin's *The Country in Her Throat*.

ACT ONE

Scene One

> *(Night. GISÈLE and YANNICK are sleeping out on the porch.)*

YANNICK: A warm breeze, the Northern Lights, you in my arms…happiness! *(A beat.)* I never saw so many stars in the sky. The most beautiful ones are in your eyes.

GISÈLE: Big silly!

YANNICK: My sweet Petunia!

GISÈLE: My handsome Puss!

YANNICK: My honey Pooh, my yummy Pooh!

GISÈLE: I'd feel more comfortable in the cottage.

YANNICK: They say the heat wave's going to last all week. We can sleep out here every night.

GISÈLE: I don't like sleeping outdoors.

YANNICK: Who says we're going to sleep?

GISÈLE: Big silly!

YANNICK: There's nothing to be afraid of. Out here, no one's going to bother us.

GISÈLE: *(Uneasy.)* I rocked my kids on this porch. My husband and I planned his retirement on this porch…

YANNICK: …but you never made love on this porch!

GISÈLE: My beautiful Puss!

YANNICK: My precious Pooh!

GISÈLE: I'm going to sleep inside.

YANNICK: I'm going to make you appreciate the outdoors!

             (They embrace.)

GISÈLE: You hear that whining noise?

YANNICK: Where?

GISÈLE: There's a mosquito.

YANNICK: I don't believe you.

GISÈLE: I hate that.

YANNICK: We're not going in.

GISÈLE: *(A beat.)* I don't hear him now.

YANNICK: What did I tell you? Now relax, let's have some peace.

GISÈLE: It's worse when you can't hear them.

YANNICK: I could eat you all over.

GISÈLE: I'll bet that's what the mosquito's thinking. He's probably rubbing his little stinger between his legs, wondering where to bite me.

YANNICK: I'll bet he doesn't even exist.

GISÈLE: What do you want to bet he's on me?

YANNICK: I'm the big mosquito! Now where shall I start? *(He gets stung.)* Ayoye!

GISÈLE: Not so loud!

YANNICK: That hurts!

GISÈLE: You see why camping out on the porch is a lousy idea? I hope the neighbours didn't hear.

YANNICK: Is that all the sympathy I get?

GISÈLE: Silly Puss!

YANNICK: Silly Petunia! Now, where was I?

               (YANNICK disappears under the covers.)

GISÈLE: No, no, stop. Not that! That tickles! Stop it, it tickles!
               Shhh, we mustn't make any noise. You're not going to
               do that, are you? I forbid it. *(A beat.)* No, go ahead, do it.
               Do it, Yannick! Yannick! Yaaaaanick!

               (We hear the sound of a buzzsaw nearby.)

YANNICK: If that's a mosquito, he must weigh three hundred
               pounds!

GISÈLE: *(Stepping on to the beach, covered in her sheet.)* Does he
               have no idea what time it is?

YANNICK: Gisèle, come back!

GISÈLE: Call the police.

YANNICK: Call the police, are you crazy? It's only six months since
               I got out of prison!

               (A sheet around his waist, he joins her on the beach.)

GISÈLE: He has no right to disturb us at this hour.

YANNICK: It doesn't disturb me. In fact, it turns me on.

GISÈLE: Yes, just like that music you're so fond of. *(We hear the
               sound of an electric drill.)* If I catch him with that drill,
               I'll bore holes in his ears! I'll make earrings out of that
               buzzsaw!

YANNICK: Come back to bed!

GISÈLE: We put up with his banging all day long. There's a limit!

YANNICK: *(Ribbing her.)* Gisèle, didn't you say that no one should
               know we're here?

GISÈLE: We're going to put up with that and do nothing?

               (We hear the blows of a hammer.)

YANNICK: Didn't you say a respectable widow like you shouldn't
             be seen with a bum like me?

GISÈLE: I'll make him swallow his nails!

YANNICK: Why not let him find out about us? He'll be the first to
             know!

GISÈLE: He'll need those tools for crutches!

YANNICK: Go on, then, give him hell!

                     (Again, the buzzsaw.)

GISÈLE: I'm going to get dressed and go over there.

YANNICK: I'll get your clothes.

GISÈLE: No! I'm not going.

YANNICK: I'm fed up with this. When your daughter showed up two
             months ago, I had to pretend I was the delivery boy. Then
             when your son arrived two weeks later, I had to be the
             gardener and start mowing the lawn...

GISÈLE: It's too soon.

YANNICK: Isn't it a drag, coming to a one-room apartment where
             there's no room to breathe? Do you like waking up with
             your nose next to the trash?

GISÈLE: Tuesdays I don't mind. It's garbage day.

YANNICK: I want people to know me as my real self!

GISÈLE: It's too soon!

YANNICK: I want to meet the people you hang out with, your
             friends!

GISÈLE: It's too soon!

YANNICK: I want your kids to call me Papa.

GISÈLE: Call you what?

YANNICK: Papa.

GISÈLE: For that, it's really too soon!

YANNICK: I'd even like to meet this guy who plays with his tools after ten o'clock. Let's go.

GISÈLE: My husband's only been dead five months. How's that going to look?

YANNICK: Like you're alive. Fred would be happy that you've fallen in love again.

GISÈLE: Wrong. Fred Cloutier would be jealous, dead or alive. I'm sure that mosquito was him.

YANNICK: Let's go!

GISÈLE: How am I going to break it to the twins?

YANNICK: *(Heavy drama.)* Children, I've something very serious to tell you... I don't know how to say this...I'm in love...and...what's worse...it's with a man. Please don't cry, I know it's tough for you.

GISÈLE: I'd never be able to.

YANNICK: It's the most beautiful thing you could tell them.

GISÈLE: It's not that simple.

YANNICK: You're afraid of what they'll think? That I'm only after your money? You've got lots, I'd be crazy not to be! *(A beat.)* You don't want them to know about my police record?

GISÈLE: Given the cases I deal with, your police record's hardly going to shock them.

YANNICK: Why, what does it say?

GISÈLE: That you're just a bum who got drunk one night and decided to steal an old '72 Buick to impress his buddies. They've seen worse.

YANNICK: My police record's not good enough?

GISÈLE: Not really.

YANNICK: I don't have a resumé, I never got a diploma, the only thing in my life I could be proud of is my police record, and she doesn't think it's good enough!

GISÈLE: No!

YANNICK: I stole others, you know. It's not my fault I only got caught once.

GISÈLE: How can I explain your age?

YANNICK: So that's it! Here we go again. What's this with my age?

GISÈLE: I'm twice your age! And when I say twice, I'm stretching it.

YANNICK: You're the most beautiful woman I know!

GISÈLE: *(To herself.)* What a crazy idea, making love in the dark!

YANNICK: You can tell them my voice has changed, my wisdom teeth have come in, I've grown hair under my arms!

GISÈLE: Don't be ridiculous.

YANNICK: You tell them, Yannick is twenty.

GISÈLE: And how will that make me look?

YANNICK: Like a woman in love!

GISÈLE: Not so loud!

YANNICK: *(Yelling it.)* I love you! *(A beat.)* Look, the older you get, the more attention you need, special treatment, tender loving care... They'll understand, what you needed was a young lover, vital, energetic...

GISÈLE: They'll think it's not serious.

YANNICK: Who?

GISÈLE: I'll be the laughing stock of the family.

YANNICK: You? You believe that? You think it's not serious? Gisèle? *(A beat.)* The plan for tonight has changed. I'm going in the lake. Maybe that'll calm me down.

                (He drops his sheet. Naked, he heads towards the lake.)

GISÈLE: You're not going swimming like that?

YANNICK: *(Off.)* If I get arrested, it'll look good on my police record!

GISÈLE: He's going in naked! This is heart attack country, I don't have a neighbour under sixty. If anyone sees him, there'll be a coronary for sure. *(Looking up.)* Wipe that grin off your face, Fred Cloutier! *(Calling.)* Where are you, Puss? Yannick? Puss?

                (NAPOLÉON enters, carrying his electric drill.)

NAPOLÉON: Can I help you, Madame Gisèle?

GISÈLE: You scared me!

NAPOLÉON: Don't tell me you've finally decided to reopen your cottage? After three years?

GISÈLE: Don't tell me you're still renovating yours. After three years?

NAPOLÉON: As things age, they require more attention, tender loving care...

GISÈLE: This is no time for that kind of talk. And it's no time to be playing with your tools.

NAPOLÉON: Jeez, you look like a goddess in that sheet. With due respect to your husband, I wouldn't mind being your bedspread. *(He chuckles to himself.)*

GISÈLE: I'll get changed.

NAPOLÉON: No, stay like that! You look gorgeous, like a statue.

GISÈLE: Seriously?

NAPOLÉON: Did you change your hair colour? Weren't you...wait a minute, you were...you were...

GISÈLE: Grey! Don't be shy, I was grey.

NAPOLÉON: I've always had a weakness for blondes. Were you looking for someone?

GISÈLE: What?

NAPOLÉON: Puss?

GISÈLE: Puss?

NAPOLÉON: That's right, Puss, Yannick? Who's that?

GISÈLE: Oh, I see. It's...my cat! I've lost my cat.

NAPOLÉON: What does he look like?

GISÈLE: He's a young Tom. He's not used to the country, he
               sleeps on the porch, goes swimming at the oddest hours.

NAPOLÉON: A cat that swims?

GISÈLE: He's imported.

NAPOLÉON: Would you like me to help you look for him?

GISÈLE: He'll come back on his own.

NAPOLÉON: Your husband's not here?

GISÈLE: No. My husband is... I'm alone.

NAPOLÉON: He's still sick?

GISÈLE: ...Not anymore.

NAPOLÉON: That's great news. I don't expect to be either. A few
               months ago I caught a little chill, but...

GISÈLE: My husband caught the big one.

NAPOLÉON: ...but now it's all better.

GISÈLE: Speaking of chills, I should get into something warmer.

NAPOLÉON: Your husband wouldn't by any chance have a five-
               eighths inch bit? It's for my drill. I'm about to install
               some oarlocks to hold the oars in place on my boat. The
               only screws I have are five-eighths. I could have sworn I
               bought three-quarter, but when I opened the box just now
               I noticed the salesman had given me the five-eighths.
               I've got bits that measure one-eighth, three-eighths, half
               inch, three quarters, one quarter...

GISÈLE: Monsieur Napoléon, I don't know what size my husband
               has.

NAPOLÉON: Are we still talking about the drill? *(He chuckles.)*

GISÈLE: Can't it wait 'til tomorrow?

NAPOLÉON: Not really.

GISÈLE: Later in the week?

NAPOLÉON: I have to finish it tonight. I put a little glue on the wood... There are several kinds, but I decided on Pine Glue, it comes from the base of the pine tree. Apparently they mix pine sawdust with a small quantity of very strong glue. They make a little paste with it... You apply the pine glue after you've installed the plank, but you have to make it really solid with screws and then bolts... The Pine Glue itself isn't strong enough to hold the plank...

GISÈLE: Monsieur Napoléon!

NAPOLÉON: If I don't put the screws in tonight, the plank will fall off. *(A beat.)* It doesn't make him anxious, your husband? To leave a lovely creature like you all alone...with her cat? As long as she was alive, I'd never have left my wife alone...no, by Jeez, I would have installed an alarm system.

GISÈLE: I didn't know you were so romantic.

NAPOLÉON: Have you seen the latest alarm systems? You can't really afford them, the price is crazy. There's the Security Safety. That you can buy. It comes in three pieces: there's a box for the lock, another for the signal, and a third for the programmer... It comes in several models... There's also the Caution-Caution; that one has twelve pieces; the first is a...

GISÈLE: Monsieur Napoléon, I'm starting to feel cold...and please, don't talk to me about heaters...

NAPOLÉON: Haven't I always said, a woman's best heater is a man's embrace?

GISÈLE: Depends on the model.

NAPOLÉON: How about a first-rate vintage model?

GISÈLE: Monsieur Napoléon!

NAPOLÉON: So you're taking a break from your little scumbags?

GISÈLE: It's a centre for delinquents!

NAPOLÉON: A scumbag's a scumbag.

GISÈLE: And narrow-minded is narrow-minded!

NAPOLÉON: I just love that tone of authority, it makes me quiver inside! I know all about scumbags. Two years ago I had my car stolen. A gorgeous '72 Buick.

GISÈLE: A '72 Buick? Would you recognize the thief?

NAPOLÉON: In the flesh? No question. I was in court with him. You won't believe this, but my scumbag, he had the same name as your cat. You should have seen the mug on him, like a killer! My beautiful Buick ended up down an eighty foot ravine.

GISÈLE: A six foot ditch.

NAPOLÉON: The little bugger was on drugs!

GISÈLE: He was under the influence of alcohol!

NAPOLÉON: There were eight of them in the car!

GISÈLE: There were three!

NAPOLÉON: Since when? Were you there?

GISÈLE: I worked on the case of the delinquent in question.

NAPOLÉON: You mean the scumbag.

GISÈLE: He had no criminal record. He's just a kid who had some kleptomaniac tendencies.

NAPOLÉON: Well, I say that anyone who can't respect the law is a scumbag!

GISÈLE: What about someone who hammers and saws at eleven at night in cottage country?

NAPOLÉON: Oh, those wicked little eyes! You sure know how to get a rise out of someone! Would you be happy if I didn't do any more work tonight?

GISÈLE: Is the Pope Polish?

NAPOLÉON:	For you, I'll stop. And I'm going to help you find your cat.
GISÈLE:	I told you, he'll come back on his own.
	(We hear a plank of wood fall in the distance.)
NAPOLÉON:	So much for the plank and the glue. I'll come back tomorrow for the bit. Will your husband be here?
GISÈLE:	No. I mean...
NAPOLÉON:	He won't be here this week?
GISÈLE:	Longer than that.
NAPOLÉON:	You mean, I'll have you all to myself, the whole week?
GISÈLE:	You realize, Monsieur Napoléon, you're talking to a repectable, married woman.
NAPOLÉON:	You're breaking my heart.
GISÈLE:	Fix it with Pine Glue.
NAPOLÉON:	You mean, on a beautiful Saturday night, all that's left for a man...
GISÈLE:	...is to turn on the Playboy channel.
NAPOLÉON:	That's right! There showing *Emmanuelle 12* again tonight. Can I tempt you?
GISÈLE:	No. Gisèle 52 has to go to bed.
NAPOLÉON:	*(Suddenly.)* Did you hear that?
GISÈLE:	What?
NAPOLÉON:	That noise.
GISÈLE:	No.
NAPOLÉON:	What's that on your beach?
GISÈLE:	I'm going to bed.
NAPOLÉON:	I think there's someone on your beach.
GISÈLE:	Where?

NAPOLÉON: Over there.

GISÈLE: *(Realizing it's YANNICK.)* Where? I don't see?

NAPOLÉON: Over there! Beside the rowboat!

GISÈLE: Must be a stump.

NAPOLÉON: A stump that moves? Look at it!

(GISÈLE looks in the opposite direction.)

GISÈLE: I don't see anything.

NAPOLÉON: Not there. There!

GISÈLE: Oh yes, I do believe...yes, it's my cat. You can go now, he's come back.

NAPOLÉON: He's built, your cat! I'd almost swear... Holy Jeez, it's a man, and...

GISÈLE: A man on my beach?

NAPOLÉON: Jesus, Mary and Joseph, he's naked!

GISÈLE: Will you stop that kind of talk! Whew, I'm hot!

NAPOLÉON: A minute ago you were cold.

GISÈLE: At my age you're like a thermostat in winter, too hot, too cold, never the right temperature.

NAPOLÉON: Look for yourself. A head, two arms, two legs... Shall I continue?

GISÈLE: You're right, it's a man. But I'm sure he's wearing a bathing suit. You know, they have flesh-coloured ones these days...

NAPOLÉON: So what's that motif on the front?

GISÈLE: Monsieur Napoléon, go and watch your film!

NAPOLÉON: *(Calling.)* Hey! Pervert!

GISÈLE: It's my beach. I'll chase him away!

NAPOLÉON: Bugger off!

GISÈLE:	He's not armed, is he?
NAPOLÉON:	*(Looking again.)* There's no way that's a gun.
GISÈLE:	*(Suddenly hoarse.)* Hey, you! Over there!
NAPOLÉON:	Louder!
GISÈLE:	You've no business being on my beach! If you don't leave I'm going to call the police. Go away!
NAPOLÉON:	He'll never hear that.
GISÈLE:	*(No voice.)* It's all your fault. You make me stand out here with nothing on but a sheet. I'm catching cold.
NAPOLÉON:	We can't have that! *(Suddenly.)* Hey, he's gone!
GISÈLE:	*(No voice.)* I suggest you do the same thing.

(Chuckling to himself, NAPOLÉON begins to unbutton his shirt.)

I meant, go!

NAPOLÉON:	I just love that bossy tone of yours. I'm going, but I'm going to keep an eye out. I'll get my shotgun, a Winchester 323, double-barrelled, Verrax telescopic lens, four-hundred metre range...
GISÈLE:	*(No voice.)* Fine, fine. Off you go!
NAPOLÉON:	If he shows up again, I'll take care of that motif on the front of his bathing suit.
GISÈLE:	*(Aside.)* My God!
NAPOLÉON:	Go and get warm, now. I don't want you losing that beautiful voice.

(NAPOLÉON exits.)

GISÈLE:	I sure as heck don't want him chasing Yannick with his shotgun. Where's he gone, anyway? *(Addressing the skies.)* That's typical of you, Fred Cloutier! Well, you know those masses I received for you? I'm not taking them to the priest, you don't deserve them! *(Calling.)* Yannick, where are you? Are you still mad at me? Come

on back, Puss... I'd better stop calling him that. *(She picks up YANNICK's sheet and breathes it in.)* If you only knew, Fred! When I look into his eyes, my hair is long again, my cheeks are firm, my complexion smooth, I smile like a girl of twenty and then all of a sudden I catch myself in the mirror...the wrinkles, the mouth that's getting smaller, my fifty-two years. He makes me feel wonderful, but I...maybe I'm fooling myself...

LOUISETTE: *(Off.)* Maman?

LOUIS: *(Off.)* Maman?

LOUISETTE: *(Off.)* Are you there, Maman?

GISÈLE: It's not possible! *(Frantically, she begins to pick up clothes from the porch.)* You keep this up, Fred Cloutier, and I won't send the thank you cards for your funeral. *(Answering LOUISETTE.)* I'm here! On the beach!

(LOUIS and LOUISETTE appear.)

LOUISETTE: You're not in bed?

GISÈLE: *(Her arms laden with clothes.)* I will be soon. I've already got my sheet on.

LOUISETTE: What's that on your head?

GISÈLE: Hair.

LOUISETTE: What happened to your beautiful grey hair?

GISÈLE: I added some blond. Makes me look younger, don't you think?

(Silence.)

LOUISETTE: Well...forty-eight, maybe.

LOUIS: Forty-five.

LOUISETTE: What are you doing with those clothes?

GISÈLE: I was about to do some laundry. Just an armful.

LOUIS: At this hour?

LOUISETTE: You keep working like that, you're going to kill yourself.

GISÈLE: Better that than die of shame.

LOUIS/
LOUISETTE: What?

LOUIS: *(Overly concerned.)* Have you been eating properly?

GISÈLE: I have.

LOUIS: Did you bring something nice to read?

GISÈLE: I did.

LOUIS: Did you bring along some fun games to play?

GISÈLE: Oh, yes!

LOUIS: Did you go for a little walk?

GISÈLE: For God's sake, Louis, how old do you think I am?

LOUIS: We feel bad we've left you alone so much since Papa died.

LOUISETTE: Can it, Louis!

GISÈLE: We don't have to stop living just because your father's dead. *(Sombre.)* It's not easy, but life goes on.

LOUISETTE: *(Lighting a cigarette.)* You're surprised to see us, eh?

             (LOUIS grabs LOUISETTE's cigarette and breaks it.)

LOUISETTE: Do you know how much that costs?

LOUIS: You want me to help you, yes or no?

LOUISETTE: Just one cigarette. One every two days?

LOUIS: No!

LOUISETTE: We found your note on the kitchen table.

GISÈLE: You forgot to read it, or you don't know how to read?

LOUISETTE: You said you were going to the cottage.

GISÈLE: And?

LOUISETTE:　That you needed to be alone...

GISÈLE:　So what are you doing here?

LOUIS:　The ashes arrived yesterday.

GISÈLE:　Ashes?

LOUISETTE:　*(Trying to shut him up.)* Louis!

LOUIS:　You know, the ashes!

GISÈLE:　The ashes?

LOUISETTE:　Louis!

LOUIS:　Papa's ashes!

GISÈLE:　*(Falsely sombre.)* Already?

LOUIS:　I had so much trouble sleeping last night. I had them with me. I could feel Papa's presence everywhere in the apartment. I decided to call Louisette this morning so that we could get rid of them...I mean...respect his last wishes...

LOUIS/
LOUISETTE:　To scatter his ashes on the blue waters of Leech Lake.

GISÈLE:　Poor leeches! I mean, you're right. That's what he wanted. *(Brushing away a false tear.)* You must excuse me.

(She goes into the cottage.)

LOUISETTE:　See that? You've made her cry. You didn't have to mention Papa the minute we got here.

LOUIS:　I didn't mention Papa. I mentioned his ashes.

LOUISETTE:　What the hell's she doing with that sheet draped around her?

LOUIS:　I can't figure out why she's doing laundry.

LOUISETTE:　And the hair? She looks like a go-go dancer who forgot to retire. Poor Maman.

LOUIS:　Condemned to solitude for the rest of her life.

LOUISETTE: Don't overdo it, Louis. Better to see her coping with a bit of solitude than sitting up with Papa night after night at the hospital.

LOUIS: Three years at the bedside of a dying man.

LOUISETTE: She'll find someone. Some great-looking guy in his sixties with gorgeous grey hair...

LOUIS: And a gorgeous pension...

LOUISETTE: And a gorgeous condo in Florida...

LOUIS: You think so? Don't forget Papa's dying words.

LOUISETTE: *(Imitating her father.)* "Take your time, Gisèle. Don't be in a hurry to replace me. Take plenty of time. Just remember, I'll be watching everything you do."

LOUIS: She's not about to find someone, just like that. Anyway, at her age...

LOUISETTE: It's got nothing to do with age. How long have you been alone?

LOUIS: Since Papa got sick. Remember what he said?

LOUISETTE: *(Imitating her father.)* "Louis, my boy, I cannot accept that you like to go out with boys. I think it's because of that I started to get sick."

LOUIS: Since then I haven't been able to get close to anyone. Haven't wanted to.

LOUISETTE: *(Imitating her father.)* "Louisette, you can go out with whoever you like. I just want you to know that when you took up with that fifty-year-old, I took a turn for the worse." *(A beat.)* Me too, I stopped wanting to.

LOUIS: We shouldn't be talking like this. Papa's still around, you know.

LOUISETTE: Not for long. Go get the ashes.

LOUIS: What for?

LOUISETTE: We're going to scatter them over the blue waters of Leech Lake.

LOUIS: *(Scandalized.)* Now? Just like that?

LOUISETTE: We should have gotten rid of them right after the funeral.

LOUIS: We had to wait for the lake to thaw!

LOUISETTE: Do you realize it's three years we've been in the dumps? I want to have some fun. I want the sun back in my life. I want a cigarette!

LOUIS: No!

LOUISETTE: I'm dying to fall in love. Aren't you?

LOUIS: *(Dreamy.)* I can see him.

LOUISETTE: Who?

LOUIS: My future mate. Young, athletic, rough...a romantic type, who likes to sleep under the stars. *(Suddenly seeing someone at the edge of the water.)* Louisette, you won't believe this, but I see him. I can see him for real, on the beach! He's young, athletic, and...he's naked!

LOUISETTE: Where?

                (NAPOLÉON enters.)

                Is that your idea of young, athletic and naked?

NAPOLÉON: *(Mysterious, with his shotgun in hand.)* Don't be alarmed, kids, I'm looking for your mother's cat.

LOUISETTE: Maman has a cat?

NAPOLÉON: An imported one.

LOUIS: What's the gun for?

NAPOLÉON: *(Mysteriously.)* I'm protecting your mother.

LOUISETTE: You're sure it's a cat, not a tiger?

NAPOLÉON: Sshhh! Goodnight!

LOUIS/
LOUISETTE: Goodnight, Monsieur Napoléon.

                (NAPOLÉON exits.)

LOUIS: I think I just saw this very stunning guy on the beach.

LOUISETTE: At Leech Lake, Louis, you only see respectable, older men.

LOUIS: With hairy white legs, and they're always dressed. That's more your style, eh?

LOUISETTE: So? Young guys are all airheads.

LOUIS: I could swear, Louisette, I wasn't dreaming.

LOUISETTE: Papa must have cast a spell on you.

LOUIS: Anyway, until Maman knows how I feel about men, I'm not falling in love again.

LOUISETTE: What stops you from telling her?

LOUIS: Look what happened when I told Papa.

LOUISETTE: Maman's more modern.

LOUIS: Modern? Remember the time I arrived at the cottage with this friend and her so-called boyfriend, who was in fact really mine?

LOUISETTE: Yes.

LOUIS: She never wanted the girl and him to sleep together. If she wouldn't even allow that, how do think she'd react to my situation?

LOUISETTE: But you got to sleep with your friend?

LOUIS: Of course! We anticipated her reaction.

LOUISETTE: Go get the ashes.

LOUIS: We're not going to do it properly?

LOUISETTE: We're going to do it while Maman's not here.

LOUIS: That's no good.

LOUISETTE: You want to see her cry?

LOUIS: I like seeing her cry! It makes me cry too.

LOUISETTE: Where's the urn?

LOUIS: We're going to do it tomorrow, in full daylight, and with her.

LOUISETTE: I just don't want you waking up tonight thinking Papa's in your room.

LOUIS: Here it won't be a problem.

LOUISETTE: Get them! Now!

                (From inside the cottage the telephone rings.)

                Louis, I want a straight answer. Did you tell Aunt Fernande we were coming to the cottage?

LOUIS: Why would I do that?

LOUISETTE: Yes or no? You know I can't stand lies.

LOUIS: Yes, I told her.

LOUISETTE: I'm going to kill you!

LOUIS: You don't kill your brother, especially not your twin. I just thought you might be missing her calls.

LOUISETTE: Two hours on the phone to find out how Maman's handling her 'bereavement'?

                (GISÈLE, dressed in a summer outfit that's a bit young for her, enters holding a cordless phone out to LOUISETTE.)

GISÈLE: It's for you. It's Fernande.

LOUISETTE: What's that you're wearing?

GISÈLE: Just something to relax in.

LOUISETTE: Relax? I look at you and I feel tense.

GISÈLE: *(Into the receiver.)* Tell her I haven't opened a vein yet.

LOUISETTE: *(Grabbing the receiver.)* You're dead, Louis Cloutier! Go and do what I asked.

(LOUIS goes out. GISÈLE, with a glance in the direction of the beach, goes back into the cottage.)

(On the phone.) Aunt Fer...Aunt Ferna...Aunt Fernande! Stop crying! No, Louis is not dead, Aunt Fernande! Calm down! Yes...Yes...Yes... She's eating, she's got some magazines and some games with her, she's even been for a walk... Yes... Yes... Yes... Yes, she's fine. Apart from walking around in a sheet with a peroxide hair job, looking like she just stepped out of a brothel, she's fine. *(Long silence. She lights another cigarette.)* Yes... Listen, Aunt...it's late and... Aunt Fern... Aunt Fer... Aunt...

(LOUIS returns with a box.)

LOUIS: Not much further, Papa, we're almost there.

LOUISETTE: Listen, Aunt... Aunt Fern... Aunt...

(She pinches LOUIS on his buttock and holds the receiver in his direction.)

LOUIS: Ayoye!

LOUISETTE: Aunt, I have to get off. Louis's hurt himself.

(She hangs up.)

LOUIS: Have you lost your marbles? I almost dropped him!

LOUISETTE: Quickly, get the urn!

LOUIS: First, there's something you have to know.

LOUISETTE: What?

LOUIS: You won't laugh at me?

LOUISETTE: If it's funny.

LOUIS: Forget it.

LOUISETTE: Tell me! I won't laugh.

LOUIS: Yesterday, when they came to deliver the urn, I was very nervous. In fact I was so nervous, I dropped it.

LOUISETTE: And?

(LOUIS opens the box and takes out a vacuum-cleaner bag.)

(Stunned.) You don't mean to say Papa's inside?

LOUIS: There was Papa everywhere. On the furniture, the rug, the plants... I couldn't sleep, I could feel his presence everywhere.

LOUISETTE: You realize Papa's in a vacuum-cleaner bag?

LOUIS: And he's not alone. There's all sorts of other stuff with him: coffee grounds, dead plants, dust balls from under the bed...

LOUISETTE: You mean you never changed the bag?

LOUIS: I was too flustered. I bought another urn this morning. I have to get him out of the bag and remove the stuff that doesn't belong with him.

LOUISETTE: We just have to empty the bag in the lake!

LOUIS: That won't work. He'll be mad at us.

LOUISETTE: He's dead, Louis!

LOUIS: I'm afraid!

LOUISETTE: And to think that what killed him was an allergy to dust!

(YANNICK runs on naked.)

YANNICK: Good evening!

LOUIS/
LOUISETTE: Good evening!

(YANNICK disappears into the cottage.)

LOUISETTE: Go get the vacuum.

LOUIS: Why?

LOUISETTE: Because we're going to get him out of here.

LOUIS: How?

LOUISETTE: Go get the vacuum!

(LOUIS heads towards the door and stops.)

LOUIS: Louisette?

LOUISETTE: What?

LOUIS: I'm going to ask you something, but don't laugh at me.

LOUISETTE: Depends on the question.

LOUIS: Forget it.

LOUISETTE: All right! I won't laugh.

LOUIS: I have a feeling I just said hello to the same guy I saw on the beach with no clothes on.

LOUISETTE: Me too, I have the same feeling.

LOUIS: It happened fast, eh?

LOUISETTE: It was like a vision.

(They sit down.)

I need a cigarette. Do you suppose we're really that desperate?

LOUIS: Why? Because we both saw a naked guy?

LOUISETTE: Could we have had a vision at the same time?

LOUIS: We're twins.

LOUISETTE: Twins are supposed to have special powers.

LOUIS: Like the power to visualize their fantasies? He was cute, eh?

LOUISETTE: A bit young...

LOUIS: Try and think of him again.

LOUISETTE: At the same time, okay?

LOUIS: Okay!

(A beat.)

YANNICK: *(Entering, dressed.)* You must be hungry. Food's on its way.

                (He disappears again into the cottage. They look at each other for a long moment.)

LOUIS: It works!

LOUISETTE: Too well. He reminds me of a delivery boy.

LOUIS: ...or someone mowing a lawn...

LOUIS/
LOUISETTE: Maman!

                (GISÈLE comes out of the cottage with a tray of sandwiches and soft drinks.)

GISÈLE: All this yelling, you two must be starving. How about a little sandwich?

LOUISETTE: Who's the naked guy we just saw?

GISÈLE: Where, sweetheart? I've got some egg, some ham, some naked...I mean, some chicken pâté.

LOUIS: Who was the vision?

GISÈLE: What vision? Do you want something to drink with that?

LOUISETTE: When I think we've been losing sleep over you being alone!

LOUIS: Sad!

LOUISETTE: Abandoned!

LOUIS: Dressed like everyone else!

LOUISETTE: And here you are with a *Playgirl* centrefold!

GISÈLE: I don't know who you're talking about.

LOUISETTE: The delivery boy?

GISÈLE: White or wholewheat?

LOUIS: The gardener?

GISÈLE:	Mustard or mayonnaise?
LOUIS/ LOUISETTE:	Maman!
GISÈLE:	Where's my head?
LOUISETTE:	That's right! Did you bleach your brains too?
GISÈLE:	You must be referring to Yannick. He's one of my clients at the rehabilitation centre!
LOUIS:	What's one of your clients doing here?
GISÈLE:	I brought a little work home from the office! *(She lets out a hollow laugh.)*
LOUISETTE:	You think we're going to swallow that?
GISÈLE:	Start with one of these egg salads. They're easier to digest.
LOUISETTE:	What's he doing here?
GISÈLE:	It's a delicate case.
LOUIS:	Tell us about it.
GISÈLE:	It's confidential.
LOUISETTE:	Maman!
GISÈLE:	*(Improvising.)* He's a young man who suffered a great deal in his childhood... It went on for years and years...
LOUISETTE:	So start a few months back.
GISÈLE:	Yannick suffers from... He suffers from...
YANNICK:	*(From behind the screen door.)* Would you like me to make a fire?
GISÈLE:	*(Whispering.)* That's it. He suffers from pyromania. He's burned down stores, offices, schools...
LOUIS:	Cottages?
YANNICK:	Do you want a fire, yes or no?

LOUIS/ LOUISETTE:	*(Panicked.)* No!
YANNICK:	Fine. *(He disappears.)*
GISÈLE:	He hates the city so much, he starts fires. We thought at the office it might be a good idea to bring him out here for a few days and see how he'd take to more natural surroundings.
LOUIS:	You're a saint, Maman.
GISÈLE:	I agreed because it would give me some company...and help me stop thinking about your father. *(She wipes away a false tear.)*
LOUIS:	A saint!
GISÈLE:	My work means a lot to me, that's all.
LOUISETTE:	And what is your work doing here without his clothes on?
GISÈLE:	The call of the wild?
LOUIS:	A saint.
LOUISETTE:	I'm sorry, Maman.
LOUIS:	You're always suspecting things, Louisette Cloutier, ridiculous things! Maman at her age with a guy thirty years her junior? *(He laughs.)* That's really stupid. *(He laughs even harder.)* Excuse me. *(Helping himself to a sandwich.)* You and him? *(More laughter. His mouth full.)* You could be his grandmother! *(He laughs again.)*
LOUISETTE:	Don't laugh while you're eating, Louis, you'll choke!
GISÈLE:	Try one of these ham, Louis!
	(LOUIS is choking.)
LOUISETTE:	Take it easy, for God's sake!
GISÈLE:	Have some of the chicken pâté too!
LOUISETTE:	Easy, Maman, you're going to kill him!

GISÈLE: *(Picking up the vacuum-cleaner bag.)* Do you always bring your garbage to the cottage?

                 (LOUISETTE grabs the bag, tosses it to LOUIS. He catches it, trying to contain the cloud of dust coming out of it.)

LOUISETTE: You're not going to introduce us to Yannick?

GISÈLE: He's not very sociable.

LOUISETTE: We've seen worse.

GISÈLE: Whatever you do, don't mention his problem. *(Calling.)* Yannick, come on out! I want you to meet my kids.

YANNICK: Be there in a sec, Pooh!

GISÈLE: He won't be long. He's in the bathroom.

LOUISETTE: What did he call you?

GISÈLE: It's so hot! I wouldn't mind a swim. I could cross the lake and back ten times.

YANNICK: *(Joining them. Long silence.)* You, you must be the twin and you, the other twin!

LOUISETTE: Swift!

YANNICK: What kind of car do you drive?

LOUIS: *(Fascinated.)* Nice to meet you, Yannick. My name's Jetta, I mean Louis. I have a Cloutier, I mean a Jetta.

LOUISETTE: I'm Louisette. I have a Sprint. You look good in clothes.

YANNICK: When I get uptight I like to take them off. I feel freer that way... You should try it.

LOUIS: *(Enthusiastic.)* Why not, we could do that, eh? I mean... I mean... No, we won't do that.

                 (Silence.)

YANNICK: We've got good-looking kids, eh? I mean... I mean, you've got good-looking kids, Gisèle.

                 (Silence.)

LOUISETTE: What do you do in life, apart from starting fires... I
              mean... I mean... Do you have a job or something?

YANNICK: A while back I tried school, but...

LOUISETTE: The school burned down?

YANNICK: No. Not enough enrollment. I also worked for a small
              company, but the company...

LOUIS: Went up in smoke?

YANNICK: Went bankrupt. Lately, I've been working in a garage.
              Well...a sort of garage.

LOUISETTE: I hope they're well insured.

GISÈLE: Talk, talk, talk. Now that the introductions are over, we
              should think of going to bed.

LOUIS: Already?

LOUISETTE: Weren't you tired earlier?

LOUIS: I got a boost of energy.

LOUISETTE: I think I know where that comes from.

GISÈLE: You two should be on your way. Aren't they something,
              my kids? Driving dozens of miles out here and back, just
              to say goodnight to me! Goodnight!

LOUIS: We came for the weekend.

YANNICK: That's great!

GISÈLE: *(False enthusiasm.)* Yes, isn't it great!

LOUIS: We have something important to do.

GISÈLE: Oh yes?

LOUIS: The ashes.

GISÈLE: Ashes?

LOUISETTE: Louis!

LOUIS: Yes, the ashes!

GISÈLE: *(Sombre.)* Oh right, the ashes!

YANNICK: If you're going to be spending the weekend, we should get to know each other.

LOUIS: That's a great idea, Yannick.

YANNICK: If you prefer, you can call me Papa.

GISÈLE: *(Suddenly talking a blue streak.)* Heavens, there's still some sandwiches! Quickly now, we can't let them go to waste. There's nothing nicer than sandwiches. I like them with white bread myself. I know it's not supposed to be healthy, but have you ever tried spreading butter on wholewheat, especially when it's cold? The harder you spread, the more it crumbles, the bread just falls apart in your hands...

LOUISETTE: What did you say we could call you?

GISÈLE: *(More and more frantic.)* There are some people who prefer butter, but believe me, it's not nearly as good as margarine. I know it's not supposed to be healthy to cut off the crusts, and it's certainly wasteful, but sandwiches are so much more attractive and tempting without them. Yannick, go and make some more!

YANNICK: The plate's still full.

GISÈLE: You don't know my kids. They'll eat a whole loaf each before going to bed.

LOUISETTE: You're making us sound like pigs!

GISÈLE: Go on, Yannick!

YANNICK: What do I make them with, my sweet Petu...

GISÈLE: My sweet lettuce, my sweet tomatoes, the sweet mayonnaise! You'll find everything in my sweet little fridge!

YANNICK: I'll add some sweet mustard!

GISÈLE: *(Aside to YANNICK.)* Just get out of here!

YANNICK: *(Spotting the vacuum-cleaner bag.)* What's this crap doing out here?

(He tosses the bag into the trash can at the side of the porch.)

LOUIS: No! Papa!!

YANNICK: *(A beat.)* I really appreciate that, Louis.

                (YANNICK goes into the cottage.)

LOUISETTE: So what's the next lie, Maman?

GISÈLE: Are you calling me a liar?

LOUISETTE: Yes!

GISÈLE: I am not in the habit of discussing my client's files with you or anyone else.

LOUIS: We'd just like to know why he wants us to call him Papa.

GISÈLE: You don't want to hear, it's a terrible story. I'm not even sure I remember how it begins.

LOUISETTE: Try going to the end.

GISÈLE: It was a long, long, long time ago... I could use a glass of wine.

LOUIS: I'll get some.

GISÈLE: Bring the bottle.

                (LOUIS goes into the cottage.)

LOUISETTE: Why don't you simply admit you're having a fling with him?

GISÈLE: I'm not having a fling with him.

LOUISETTE: We'd understand.

GISÈLE: Yannick is a client!

LOUISETTE: You sure it's not you that's the client?

GISÈLE: Louisette Cloutier!

LOUISETTE: Some women get taken to the cleaners by young gigolos.

GISÈLE: You've been watching too many sex-talk shows!

LOUISETTE: Mature women, recently widowed, are their favourite targets. I think Yannick fits the bill...

GISÈLE: You ought to know that at my age one doesn't fall for a man like that. Never mind that he's got eyes that would make any woman weak and a smile that would make their hearts turn somersaults, or hands as tender as satin, that's not what interests me. I'm totally indifferent to all that.

LOUIS: *(Returning with the bottle of wine.)* Yannick is really interesting!

GISÈLE: *(After taking a large swig from the bottle.)* Yannick set his parents' house on fire. *(She takes another swig.)* His father died in the fire. Ever since then he's wanted people to call him Papa to alleviate some of the guilt he feels over his father's death.

LOUIS: This is a monster!

GISÈLE: That's right, Louis, a monster. And that's not half of it. You should see his police record: thick as a phone book. You name it, he's done it!

               (YANNICK returns with the ingredients for the sandwiches.)

YANNICK: I hope you've got everything you need.

LOUIS: Yannick... I mean, Papa!

LOUISETTE: *(Nodding.)* Papa!

LOUIS: Maman's explained everything.

YANNICK: Wasn't that complicated, was it, Gisèle?

LOUISETTE: She told us everything.

YANNICK: You're not taking it very well.

LOUIS: What?!?

YANNICK: So far, I have no regrets.

LOUISETTE:	That's appalling!
YANNICK:	I know it's not that common, it's something people aren't really cool with, but to me, it's beautiful.
LOUIS:	It's monstrous!
YANNICK:	Crazy, maybe, but beautiful! Passionate, fiery...
LOUIS:	No remorse!
YANNICK:	Why? *(Seeing that GISÈLE is about to empty the bottle.)* Gisèle, you're going to get drunk!
LOUIS:	I've heard enough. I'm going to bed. Come on, Louisette, let's get the bags.

(They exit.)

YANNICK:	Feeling better, now that you've told them? *(Silence.)* Petunia?
GISÈLE:	Petunias belong in the window box. Don't call me that anymore!
YANNICK:	You don't have to be ashamed just 'cause you told them we love each other. It's a shock, but they'll get over it.
GISÈLE:	I've no idea how many lies I've told tonight. I just wish I could remember.
YANNICK:	What lies?
GISÈLE:	The twins still don't know anything about us.
YANNICK:	What do they know?
GISÈLE:	Stuff I've invented about your past.
YANNICK:	What stuff?
GISÈLE:	You'll find out for yourself. Good luck.
YANNICK:	Did I do something wrong?
GISÈLE:	Papa!?
YANNICK:	Okay, it was a bit soon, but... What are the lies about my past?

GISÈLE: I suggest you agree with everything they tell you about your monstrous life.

YANNICK: You're punishing me.

GISÈLE: The twins will sleep in their respective beds, I in mine...

YANNICK: And me?

GISÈLE: On the porch!

YANNICK: You really don't want them to know.

GISÈLE: I don't want my family, my relations, my neighbours having anything to do with my love life, is that clear? You're the most wonderful secret I ever had in my life, and I intend to keep it!

YANNICK: And I thought teenagers were complicated!

             (He takes the bottle from GISÈLE.)

             I'm going for a walk.

GISÈLE: Keep your clothes on!

             (YANNICK exits.)

             Fred Cloutier, I'll bet you're busting a gut! If you don't stop interfering, I'm going to dump your ashes in the barbecue. *(A beat.)* Now, no more lies, Gisèle. Not one!

             (LOUISETTE has returned with her bags. NAPOLÉON runs on with a cat in his hands.)

NAPOLÉON: Madame Gisèle, Madame Gisèle, I think I've found Yannick!

GISÈLE: *(No voice.)* That's not him, Monsieur Napoléon, that's not him.

LOUISETTE: Yannick?

             (Blackout.)

Scene Two

(Thunder and distant lightning. LOUISETTE iptoes out of the cottage in her nightie and takes a cigarette from her pack.)

LOUISETTE: It's my last! *(Reading from the package.)* "Tobacco smoke causes lung disease in non-smokers." How depressing can you get? One day the print will be so big, you'll have to ask for "A Fatal Lung Disease for Non-Smokers, please!" Not my problem... *(She goes to toss the empty pack in the trash can.)* Are you okay, Papa? It's not very considerate, I know, but in the trash can nobody will suspect a thing. You never wanted me to smoke...You knew I was pig-headed, it's all your fault! You should have said, "Smoke, Louisette, smoke!" I would have done the opposite!

(A clap of thunder. LOUISETTE sees YANNICK approaching, and quickly goes to hide. YANNICK enters, shivering and soaking wet.)

YANNICK: *(At the door.)* Gisèle, open up! Let me in!

GISÈLE: *(Behind the screen door.)* What happened to your heat wave?

YANNICK: What's that on your face?

GISÈLE: Yoghurt.

YANNICK: Did you have an accident? Isn't there a light in your fridge? *(Pause.)* It's been raining.

GISÈLE: You woke me up to tell me it's been raining?

YANNICK: I'm soaked!

GISÈLE: I'm not.

YANNICK:	I'm freezing!
GISÈLE:	I'm not.
YANNICK:	I'm going to catch cold!
GISÈLE:	Too bad.
YANNICK:	Let me in!
GISÈLE:	No way.
YANNICK:	Gisèle, let me in!
GISÈLE:	Good night!
YANNICK:	I'm sorry I asked your kids to call me Papa.
GISÈLE:	That's all?
YANNICK:	Don't be so mean!
GISÈLE:	Sweet dreams!
YANNICK:	Okay, I'll pretend everything you said about my past is true.
GISÈLE:	*(She opens the door.)* That's better. Don't make a sound.
YANNICK:	I'll be quiet as a cat.
GISÈLE:	Anything else, but not a cat!

(She dries his head with a towel.)

Where are you going to sleep?

YANNICK:	In your arms.
GISÈLE:	I didn't hear that.
YANNICK:	In your arms!
GISÈLE:	You're going to sleep on the sofa.
YANNICK:	The sofa's too small. Why not with you?
GISÈLE:	After they've gone.
YANNICK:	You mean we can't sleep together all weekend?

GISÈLE: It's not easy for me either.

YANNICK: You could tell them the truth.

GISÈLE: Do you want to sleep out here?

               (A beat.)

YANNICK: May I kiss you?

GISÈLE: If you like blueberries.

YANNICK: *(Licking her face.)* I'm going to eat you up!

GISÈLE: The rest of the container's in the fridge. Yannick, stop!
               It's for my wrinkles.

YANNICK: What wrinkles?

GISÈLE: Here, in my face! Like the highways of Quebec!

YANNICK: Don't mention highways or cars... I get too excited!

GISÈLE: Time for bed.

YANNICK: Already? I was saving that yummy patch just below your
               eye there. Gisèle, you know what?

GISÈLE: What?

YANNICK: *(Whispering.)* I love you!

GISÈLE: Big silly!

YANNICK: My sweet Petunia!

GISÈLE: My handsome Puss!

YANNICK: My yummy Pooh!

               *(A clap of thunder. They exit into the cottage.
               LOUISETTE reappears.)*

LOUISETTE: "My yummy Pooh!" "My handsome Puss!" *(She opens
               the trash can.)* What does she think we are, Papa, idiots?
               I'm going to get to the bottom of this!

               (Blackout.

               End of ACT ONE.)

ACT TWO

Scene One

	(Six o'clock the following morning. Superb weather. Birdsong. All is calm and serene. NAPOLÉON enters with a plank of wood and his power saw. He plugs in the saw and proceeds To cut the plank.)
GISÈLE:	*(Coming out of the cottage draped in a sheet, and now with red hair.)* Monsieur Napoléon!
NAPOLÉON:	You've got your voice back?
GISÈLE:	Monsieur Napoléon!
NAPOLÉON:	Did your cat come home?
GISÈLE:	Monsieur Napoléon!!!
NAPOLÉON:	You've changed your hair colour again. I hate to say it, but all that dye's going to burn your scalp!
	(She unplugs the power saw.)
	You look fantastic in that sheet! Last night in the movie—you know, *Emmanuelle 12?*—there were all these gorgeous women dressed only in sheets, and at one point they all got wet, and they looked even more gorgeous! *(Admiring GISÈLE.)* It's too bad, eh, I hear the sun's going to shine all day.
GISÈLE:	Do you know what time it is?
NAPOLÉON:	Six twelve precisely, Madame Gisèle, and you can count on my watch, it's never wrong. It's a Rolex: waterproof, anti-shock, quartz dial, twelve or twenty-four hour indicator. Has a chronometer too, measures from a

hundredth of a second up to thirty hours, a thirty-day memory, starts automatically. Ask me something and I'll time it.

GISÈLE: *(Pointing to the lake.)* How about going underwater for half an hour?

NAPOLÉON: It's supposed to go up to thirty-four today. The beach will be full of beautiful girls in bikinis.

GISÈLE: I don't wear one.

NAPOLÉON: In that case, it's going to be one helluva day!

GISÈLE: Would you mind telling me what you're doing with all your tools on my porch at six twelve...

NAPOLÉON: Thirteen! Well, last night I noticed your porch was leaning to one side.

GISÈLE: My porch is perfectly straight.

NAPOLÉON: Come over here and see. *(He places his level on the porch.)* You see that little bubble? Now, do you see what it's doing? Look at the little bugger. Come in a bit closer.

GISÈLE: I can see fine from here.

NAPOLÉON: But do you see what it's doing?

GISÈLE: Monsieur Napoléon, I have enough on my mind without worrying about the behaviour of some little bubble. I like my porch the way it is. With a bit of wood here and there and a fresh coat of paint, it'll be as good as new.

NAPOLÉON: Ah, but old things need more than cosmetic attention.

GISÈLE: That's comforting to know.

NAPOLÉON: Don't be shy, let me give you a hand!

(He plugs in the saw and starts it up again.)

GISÈLE: Monsieur Napoléon, the kids are sleeping!

NAPOLÉON: Come here and hold the plank.

GISÈLE: You're not serious!

NAPOLÉON: Come on! *(Furious, she obliges. He saws off a piece.)*
             The sound of a buzz saw, I couldn't do without it. It's like
             a song.

GISÈLE: Look, you're sweet to do this, but wouldn't it be better
             later on?

NAPOLÉON: *(He stops sawing.)* You think I'm sweet?

GISÈLE: Monsieur Napoléon, you're a dear!

NAPOLÉON: One more word like that, and before the day's over,
             you'll have yourself a new deck.

GISÈLE: Then be a love, and wait 'til noon before you start
             rebuilding my cottage.

NAPOLÉON: Be a what?

GISÈLE: A love!

NAPOLÉON: *(Setting his chronometer.)* I'll be here at noon, on the dot,
             raring to go!

GISÈLE: That's right, noon!

             *(He goes off. LOUIS comes out of the cottage with a
             sieve, a pot, and a small box.)*

             Good morning, Louis.

LOUIS: *(Seeing his mother's red hair.)* It's…beautiful… Our
             busy beaver's gone?

GISÈLE: He'll be back at noon. Our porch has a personality
             conflict with a bubble.

LOUIS: Huh?

GISÈLE: You're early.

LOUIS: I've a lot of work to do.

GISÈLE: What's in the box?

LOUIS: The thank you cards.

GISÈLE: Thank you cards?

LOUIS: You know, for Papa's death.

GISÈLE: There are people to thank for Papa's death? *(A beat.)* No
                sense of humour this morning?

LOUIS: I didn't close my eyes all night.

GISÈLE: Too many sandwiches?

LOUIS: No. Yannick came to sleep in my bed.

GISÈLE: Really?

LOUIS: He's a restless sleeper, eh?

GISÈLE: Oh, yes, and at times it's so bad...

LOUIS: Yes, so bad...

GISÈLE: So bad? Aha, so he's a restless sleeper? I never noticed
                that in his file. I'm going back to bed. *(She goes into the
                cottage.)*

                *(LOUIS removes the bag of ashes from the trash can.
                He doesn't see NAPOLÉON, who has returned to
                measure the porch.)*

LOUIS: Here we go, Papa. My God, you don't smell so good this
                morning! Did you find some friends in the garbage? That
                can of tomato juice certainly seems to like you. It won't
                be much longer. I'm going to get you out of there, but
                you have to help. *(He positions the pot and sieve
                underneath the bag.)* Now, when I squeeze the bag, I
                want you to push as well. I'll be catching you with the
                sieve, and that way we're going to remove all the bad
                things that don't belong with you.

NAPOLÉON: Who are you talking to, Louis?

LOUIS: *(Startled.)* You nearly scared me to death!

NAPOLÉON: Who are you talking to?

LOUIS: My father.

NAPOLÉON: Where is he?

LOUIS: In the bag.

NAPOLÉON: Really? Hi, there, Fred!

LOUIS: Don't tell Maman.

NAPOLÉON: I'd have to be crazy before I'd tell that to your mother.

LOUIS: You don't understand?

NAPOLÉON: I understand you've got a screw loose!

LOUIS: Our father died, five months ago.

NAPOLÉON: Sure! And I do embroidery in my spare time. What do you take me for? Last night your mother told me your father was in perfect health.

LOUIS: She must have been telling stories.

NAPOLÉON: Well, between you talking to a vacuum-cleaner bag, and your mother, I prefer to believe her.

LOUIS: Maman told you he was still alive? *(Handing him one of the thank-you cards.)* Read that!

NAPOLÉON: "Madame Gisèle Gélinas-Cloutier and her children, Louisette and Louis, wish to thank you, dear..." Dear who?

LOUIS: You have to write the name of whoever you're sending it to.

NAPOLÉON: "...on the occasion of the death...of Alfred Cloutier." *(A beat.)* And the bag?

LOUIS: There was an accident and I had to pick him up with the vacuum cleaner.

NAPOLÉON: Jesus, Mary, and Joseph! What sort of accident? 'Cause to pick up someone with a vacuum you'd have beat him to a pulp!

LOUIS: His ashes, Monsieur Napoléon. His ashes got dropped after the cremation.

NAPOLÉON: Then why are you passing them through a sieve?

LOUIS: So they'll be clean when they get thrown in the lake.

NAPOLÉON: Poor Fred, if he's reincarneated, he'll be one helluva mess!

LOUIS: After we've scattered him in Leech Lake, he'll be at peace, and so will I.

NAPOLÉON: Wait a minute. If your father's dead, that means your mother's a widow.

LOUIS: Absolutely.

NAPOLÉON: That means she's free? Holy Jeez, is it ever going to be a beautiful day!

(He gathers up his tools in a hurry. Inside the cottage, the telephone rings.)

LOUIS: What's the big hurry all of a sudden?

NAPOLÉON: *(Pointing to the cottage.)* You see there? We're going to have a row of six windows, Perglass-Thermo. On the roof, some slate tiles, and over there…that's going to be the most beautiful extension between two cottages you ever saw! I'm inspired, I have to go to the hardware.

(He exits. A sleepy LOUISETTE comes out of the cottage, talking on the phone.)

LOUISETTE: That's right, Aunt… Yes… Aunt Fern… Aunt Fer… Aunt Fer… *(She pinches LOUIS.)*

LOUIS: Ayoye!

LOUISETTE: I'll call you later. Louis's hurt himself again. *(She hangs up.)*

LOUIS: That hurt!

LOUISETTE: Monsieur Napoléon's gone already?

LOUIS: He went to the hardware store.

LOUISETTE: I can't wait to see him again. There's something about him…

LOUIS: I never thought a box of tools would turn you on.

LOUISETTE: What's he up to?

LOUIS:	He's going to build an extension between our cottages.
LOUISETTE:	A what?
LOUIS:	Maman never told him Papa was dead. When he found out she was a widow, it rekindled his flame.
LOUISETTE:	Speaking of flames, where's Yannick?
LOUIS:	Sleeping.
LOUISETTE:	Really? Where?
LOUIS:	I've brought the thank-you cards.
LOUISETTE:	Whose bed did he sleep in?
LOUIS:	We have to fill them out and post them.
LOUISETTE:	Take a valium! What's the rush? *(She takes one of the cards.)* Good grief, was he in his coffin when you took this picture?
LOUIS:	What's wrong with it?
LOUISETTE:	Nobody's going to miss him looking like that.
LOUIS:	The photo has to be serious. If the dead person's smiling in one of these, it's like you're saying, "Don't worry, your turn's next!"
LOUISETTE:	You should have used another one.
LOUIS:	You should have taken care of it!
LOUISETTE:	My, we're in a swell mood this morning!
LOUIS:	After the night I've just been through…
LOUISETTE:	So…? *(She starts filling in the thank-you cards.)*
LOUIS:	You won't laugh?
LOUISETTE:	If it's funny…
LOUIS:	Forget it.
LOUISETTE:	I won't laugh.

LOUIS:　　　　　Yannick slept with me.

LOUISETTE:　　Did you take some precaution? Did you use a...

LOUIS:　　　　　He was all over the place, clinging, pawing, muttering all this mush...

LOUISETTE:　　What was he saying?

LOUIS:　　　　　My sweet Petunia, my yummy Pooh...

LOUISETTE:　　I'll bet you liked that.

LOUIS:　　　　　Give me a break!

LOUISETTE:　　My God, you idiot!

LOUIS:　　　　　What?

LOUISETTE:　　Can you believe it? I've written, "...wish to thank you, dear Pooh!"

LOUIS:　　　　　Don't waste them. I don't have any extras.

LOUISETTE:　　And did you...did you need a...well, you know what I mean.

LOUIS:　　　　　He was asleep, Louisette!

LOUISETTE:　　Which means, you didn't have to use a...

LOUIS:　　　　　I don't know if he's...

LOUISETTE:　　Ah, you don't know if... I thought your instinct was foolproof.

LOUIS:　　　　　If we could trust our instinct, Louisette, there'd be a lot less heartbreak, and fewer black eyes!

LOUISETTE:　　You should try and find out.

LOUIS:　　　　　Until Maman knows about me, no relationship.

LOUISETTE:　　But if you had done it, you would have used a...

LOUIS:　　　　　Yes, I would have used a...

LOUISETTE:　　I'm such an idiot!

LOUIS: What?

LOUISETTE: Look, I've written, "wish to thank you, dear condom!"

LOUIS: Stop wasting them! Now we'll have to decide who's not going to get one.

LOUIS/
LOUISETTE: *(After a beat.)* Aunt Fernande! *(They laugh.)*

LOUIS: She was so embarrassing at the funeral home. She cried so hard, you'd have thought she was the widow, that she'd spent every day of her life with him.

LOUISETTE: Not every day, maybe, but the odd night.

LOUIS: You don't mean that...

LOUISETTE: Why do you think she phones here all the time?

LOUIS: Does Maman know?

LOUISETTE: She's known for ages. Our aunt wants her big sister to forgive her.

LOUIS: You can tell me that in front of Papa's remains, like it's nothing?

LOUISETTE: You want to know the best? Last night I overheard a conversation between Maman and Yannick. Maman's also called Petunia!

LOUIS: I don't believe you!

LOUISETTE: Maman's an accomplished liar.

LOUIS: I forbid you to call her that!

LOUISETTE: Yannick was eating yoghurt off Maman's face, blueberry yoghurt!

LOUIS: Aunt Fernande and our "perfect" father used to sleep together, you've got your eye on the King of Repairmen, and if that's not enough, Yannick eats blueberry yoghurt off Maman's face? *(Exasperated.)* Have a smoke, Louisette, and if it'll keep you from hallucinating, have two!

LOUISETTE:	You're driving me nuts with your sieve. Hand me the bag. And the pot. I've got a better idea.

> *(She opens the door of the cottage. YANNICK comes out wearing only a pair of shorts and carrying a bottle of suntan lotion.)*

YANNICK: 'Morning, Louisette.

LOUISETTE: Good morning, "Papa!"

YANNICK: Where are you going with the garbage?

LOUISETTE: What's it to you, "Papa?"

YANNICK: I don't know how to light the stove.

LOUISETTE: You know, this cottage, even if we don't come here often, we're really fond of it. I'll take care of the stove.

YANNICK: Fine.

LOUISETTE: Be nice to Louis. The morning after, he's especially sensitive.

YANNICK: Huh?

> *(She disappears. YANNICK applies suntan lotion. LOUIS writes his cards.)*

It's hot already! Did you sleep okay?

LOUIS: No. Did you?

YANNICK: No problem. Did I move around a lot?

LOUIS: Yes. A lot.

YANNICK: You were hot.

LOUIS: Pardon?

YANNICK: Your body was hot.

LOUIS: I'm sorry.

YANNICK: It wasn't unpleasant.

LOUIS: *(Aside.)* Get thee behind me, Satan!

YANNICK: Since I got drenched in the rain, I was frozen, and your bed was nice and warm. Do you mind putting some oil on my back?

LOUIS: You want me to... Isn't it a bit early for that? We hardly know each other... I mean... Sitting in the sun's become very dangerous... I mean...

YANNICK: Apart from moving a lot, I didn't do anything else? *(LOUIS nods his head in the affirmative.)* I didn't try to... Damn it, I should have slept by myself. You've nothing to say?

LOUIS: You must have been popular in prison.

YANNICK: So I did try... But I only tried? I'm sorry.

LOUIS: So am I. *(Aside.)* Maman's going to find out sooner or later. Go for it, Louis! *(To YANNICK.)* Pass me the stuff.

> *(He proceeds to oil YANNICK's back. Enter LOUISETTE.)*

LOUISETTE: Louis, I need to know... *(Seeing them.)* Excuse me!

LOUIS: *(His voice suddenly macho, and rubbing very hard.)* Have you seen the new four-by-four? It's got a wicked chassis.

YANNICK: Yeah, I already stole one... I mean, had one.

LOUIS: Those ten-wheelers, do they still have the hydraulic problems they used to have? You wanted to know something, Louisette?

LOUISETTE: Nothing I'm not learning about here. *(A beat.)* I wanted you to come and help me with the ashes, but I'll let you get on with your activity.

YANNICK: Not so hard, you're going to wreck my back!

LOUIS: It has to penetrate!

LOUISETTE: Don't forget to use a...

> *(She disappears.)*

YANNICK: Did I say anything in my sleep?

LOUIS: Who's Petunia?

YANNICK: A friend. I can't tell you her name.

LOUIS: Louisette thinks it's Maman.

YANNICK: No! No, it's someone whose name I really can't reveal. It's awkward.

LOUIS: That's what I thought. To make sure no one would find out, I gave them girl's names too.

YANNICK: Huh?

LOUIS: It must have been tough, eh, your childhood?

YANNICK: What?

LOUIS: When you found out your father was dead after setting fire to the house, how did you feel?

YANNICK: My father? The house?

LOUIS: You can tell me. We've got things in common.

YANNICK: In common?

LOUIS: I think your bod's pretty hot too.

YANNICK: *(Disengaging himself.)* That's enough oil for now, thanks.

LOUIS: Maman told us everything.

YANNICK: Oh yeah?

LOUIS: Your mother... It must have been difficult for her, eh?

YANNICK: *(Lying.)* Only for a few seconds.

LOUIS: You mean your mother also...

YANNICK: The firemen only managed to save Nicole's dog and Lorraine's budgy.

LOUIS: Nicole? Lorraine?

YANNICK: They were my sisters.

LOUIS:	And they let you loose to sleep with whoever you like?
YANNICK:	Terrible, isn't it.

(NAPOLÉON enters.)

NAPOLÉON:	Louis, go and tell your mother I've found Yannick.
YANNICK:	The '72 Buick! *(He throws himself to the ground, face to the sand.)*
LOUIS:	Maman, Monsieur Napoléon has found...who?
NAPOLÉON:	Little Yannick! He's adorable, especially when you stroke him a bit.
LOUIS:	Monsieur Napoléon?
NAPOLÉON:	Don't you like to stroke them sometimes?
LOUIS:	Monsieur Napoléon!
NAPOLÉON:	Most of my neighbours prefer dogs...
LOUIS:	*(Scandalized.)* At Leech Lake?
NAPOLÉON:	But I just love pussies!
LOUIS:	Let me get this straight. You're telling me you like to "stroke" Yannick, but a few minutes ago you were all hot to build an extension between you and Maman?
YANNICK:	*(Head in the sand.)* A what?
LOUIS:	An extension.
YANNICK:	over my dead body!
NAPOLÉON:	You have a visitor? How do you do, my name's Napoléon Bonneau. You're...?
LOUIS:	You don't recognize him? I think he's got a cramp.
NAPOLÉON:	Should I recognize him?
LOUIS:	Don't be shy on my account.

(From inside the cottage we hear the sound of the vacuum.)

NAPOLÉON: *(Continuing with his story.)* Well anyway, I've got him
               in my cottage.

LOUIS: Who?

NAPOLÉON: The cat your mother lost last night. "Yannick."

LOUIS: Maman told you Yannick was her cat?

               *(We hear a cry from LOUISETTE from inside. The
               sound of the vacuum cleaner cuts out. A stunned
               LOUISETTE comes out onto the porch covered with
               ashes. GISÈLE comes out after her, wearing a green
               face pack. Seeing her mother, LOUISETTE lets out
               another cry.)*

               Louisette! Say it isn't so!

GISÈLE: What's this with the vacuum cleaner at six-thirty...

NAPOLÉON: Thirty-one...

GISÈLE: What are you doing here? Is your chronometer broken? I
               told you noon!

NAPOLÉON: What's that on your face?

GISÈLE: A beauty mask.

NAPOLÉON: Are you sure you read the instructions properly?

GISÈLE: The house is full of dust!

LOUIS: We wanted to surprise you with a nice clean cottage, eh,
               Louisette? *(She doesn't reply.)*

GISÈLE: You two are full of surprises. Good grief, Louisette, you
               look like you've just seen your father's ghost.

LOUIS: He's never been so close, that's for sure. Shall we go and
               clean up, Louisette?

LOUISETTE: I need a cigarette!

LOUIS: Haven't you had your fill of ashes?

NAPOLÉON: I think the vacuum cleaner's got something to do with
               your husband...

LOUIS:	Monsieur Napoléon!
NAPOLÉON:	The vacuum… the bag…the ashes…
GISÈLE:	I didn't know the sun struck so early. Buy yourself a hat, Monsieur Napoléon.
NAPOLÉON:	So your husband's not taking a vacation? He's going to kill himself with all that work!
GISÈLE:	*(Uneasy.)* He had a big contract to settle.
YANNICK:	*(Head still to the ground.)* Another lie, Gisèle. Cut it out!
GISÈLE:	Where's that voice coming from?
LOUISETTE:	Not your conscience, that's for sure!
NAPOLÉON:	It comes from the man on your beach. We haven't been introduced yet. I just came to tell you that I think I've found your Yannick, and…
GISÈLE:	Come inside. There's some nice sandwiches from last night.
YANNICK:	*(Getting up.)* Enough lies! Hello, Monsieur Bonneau!
NAPOLÉON:	Holy Jeez, it's my scumbag!
GISÈLE:	Delinquent!
LOUIS:	No, I believe it's your cat!
NAPOLÉON:	What's he doing here?
GISÈLE:	None of your business!
YANNICK:	What am I doing here? I'm here for a romantic weekend.
NAPOLÉON/ LOUISETTE/ LOUIS:	With who?
	(A beat.)
YANNICK:	I don't know anymore!
NAPOLÉON:	You had me believe your husband was alive when he was dead, you made me believe you had a cat called

Yannick... I was all set to build you a gorgeous extension. I'm disappointed in you, Madame Gisèle.

(NAPOLÉON leaves.)

LOUIS: We'll go and tidy up, okay, Louisette?

GISÈLE: Don't touch a thing in there. A little hot water and some Mister Clean...

LOUIS: No!!

GISÈLE: What's wrong with Mister Clean?

YANNICK: What a body, though! And that little earring's so trendy.

LOUIS: Listen, Mr. Sandpaper Number 3, just give it a rest! *(To GISÈLE.)* We'll clean up our own mess.

LOUISETTE: Poor Monsieur Napoléon!

LOUIS: Come on!

(LOUIS and LOUISETTE exit into the cottage.)

GISÈLE: I'm purple with shame.

YANNICK: Don't worry, there's so much gunk on your face, it doesn't show.

GISÈLE: You're not going to kiss me?

YANNICK: Where? I'll kiss you when you've told them the truth.

GISÈLE: It's too soon!

YANNICK: I wonder if someone's left the keys in their car?

GISÈLE: Where are you going?

YANNICK: To steal a car. Lies and I don't get on together.

GISÈLE: I'll tell them at noon! No, at four o'clock...

YANNICK: Why not right now? By the way, this fire that destroyed my family home? My mother and sisters also died.

GISÈLE: I never knew that.

YANNICK: It's not funny, Gisèle. And last night in my sleep, I jumped your son!

GISÈLE: Well, you were crazy to sleep in his bed. You know how restless you are at night.

YANNICK: The sofa was too small!

GISÈLE: Poor Louis, you must have scared him.

YANNICK: Scared him? My God, mothers! Gisèle, your neighbour thought I was a cat, your kids think I've done away with my family, your son thinks I prefer guys. I'm beginning to have serious identity problems!

GISÈLE: *(Smiling.)* So we don't have to make up any more lies.

YANNICK: That's not funny, Gisèle.

GISÈLE: It's too soon!

YANNICK: When you've told them, let me know.

GISÈLE: I have to prepare myself!

YANNICK: For what?

GISÈLE: It's not easy!

YANNICK: You think it's any easier for me?

GISÈLE: Don't say that!

YANNICK: I'm going to tell you something I probably shouldn't. *(Dead serious.)* It's not my age you're frightened of, it's your own.

GISÈLE: *(Hurt.)* You think I'm old? Is that it?

YANNICK: You're trying so hard to look young, you're making yourself ugly. When it's not some weird glop on your face, there's a new wig on your head.

GISÈLE: Not so loud! No one's noticed. *(A beat.)* I knew it couldn't last. Get your things and go.

YANNICK: Fine. I'll get my things, and I'll go. *(Silence.)* I love you!

GISÈLE: Don't talk that way now.

YANNICK: Will you at least tell me once that you love me?

GISÈLE: It's too soon!

YANNICK: I'm out of here.

GISÈLE: That's right, go! It's better that way. *(She goes into the cottage in tears.)*

YANNICK: Women! It's always the same, whether they're twenty, thirty or fifty...their plots, their flirting, always worrying what people will say. Well, that does it! I've had it with women!

                (LOUISETTE, dressed for the beach, comes out of the cottage.)

                You look good in that outfit!

LOUISETTE: Ben Hur, stop your chariot!

YANNICK: Can't you tell a girl she looks good without her imagining things?

LOUISETTE: With you, no imagination's needed. Sweet words, compliments, pet names like Pooh and Petunia, and you think we're yours for the taking, like apples in autumn. Your charm may work on my mother and brother, but not with me.

YANNICK: What are you talking about?

LOUISETTE: I don't like liars and hypocrites.

YANNICK: Neither do I.

LOUISETTE: I don't like watching my twin suffer.

YANNICK: I didn't mean it.

LOUISETTE: You've upset him so much, his tears are lifting the label off Mister Clean.

YANNICK: I was sleeping!

LOUISETTE: I hate seeing my mother suffer.

YANNICK: She's suffering?

LOUISETTE: She was a real mess when she came in.

YANNICK: Really?

LOUISETTE: She had these great big tears running down her face pack.

YANNICK: *(Affected.)* How awful!

LOUISETTE: No, it's disgusting! And you know what's even worse? I can't smoke!

YANNICK: I've got something important to tell you.

LOUISETTE: Let's have it.

YANNICK: You won't laugh?

LOUISETTE: If it's funny.

YANNICK: Forget it.

LOUISETTE: Go on, I won't laugh.

YANNICK: I've been involved with your mother the past two months.

LOUISETTE: I know. I caught you licking her yoghurt last night.

YANNICK: I always wanted you to know, but Gisèle refused.

LOUISETTE: Why?

YANNICK: At first I thought it was because you'd be shocked. Then I figured it had to do with my police record.

LOUISETTE: If I was sleeping with a firebug I certainly wouldn't brag about it—

YANNICK: I never started fires and I didn't kill anyone.

LOUISETTE: More of her lies?

YANNICK: I think it's to do with her age, but I'm not sure... It's like there's something else. I've had so little experience with women I don't know how to talk to them.

LOUISETTE: She's not your first girl?

YANNICK: I said I don't know how to talk to women, not girls.

LOUISETTE: A woman for you is how old?

YANNICK: At least forty.

LOUISETTE: Before that?

YANNICK: They're just girls. No life experience, and they think they know everything. It's pathetic!

LOUISETTE: You're right, you don't know how to talk to women.

YANNICK: I'd like to tell her that I love those little bags under her eyes, that I'm crazy about her crow's feet...

LOUISETTE: You mean the way she walks?

YANNICK: No, no...

LOUISETTE: It's fun to tease a lover, you know that, Yannick?

YANNICK: *(Not hearing her.)* And best of all are her eyes...

LOUISETTE: Yannick?

YANNICK: ...sometimes her eyes are like a little girl's...

LOUISETTE: Yannick?

YANNICK: ...and sometimes they're really sexy!

LOUISETTE: Yannick? Love doesn't just make you blind, it makes you deaf.

YANNICK: Every time I ask why she doesn't want you to know about us, we end up fighting.

LOUISETTE: Look, I know I'm not a real woman yet, and I think I know everything, but I'm going to help you.

YANNICK: What have you got in mind?

LOUISETTE: I'm going to invent a wonderful white lie...

YANNICK: Again? It runs in the family?

LOUISETTE: You are going to console her.

YANNICK: We've just had a fight, and she thinks I've left.

LOUISETTE: That's even better!

YANNICK: What's your idea?

LOUISETTE: Go and cool your jets somewhere for a few hours. I'll take care of everything.

YANNICK: Where should I go?

LOUISETTE: Go buy me some cigarettes!

(YANNICK leaves. NAPOLÉON enters, waving his plan for the deck.)

NAPOLÉON: Tell me honestly, Louisette, I need to know right away.

(He shows her the plan.)

Do you think she'll like it?

LOUISETTE: What's it for?

NAPOLÉON: It's a deck...with flower boxes, a place to barbecue, built-in benches, a table, patio lights, a chaise longue made of some beautiful polished wood, a little sandbox for the cats...

LOUISETTE: We don't have a cat.

NAPOLÉON: What about the two Yannicks at my place?

LOUISETTE: What's that?

NAPOLÉON: It's a wooden stool for reaching the clothes-line. You think she'll like it?

LOUISETTE: Who?

NAPOLÉON: Your mother!

LOUISETTE: You're not going to build the extension?

NAPOLÉON: Since she's found her young friend, I've sort of lost interest. Do you think she'll like it?

LOUISETTE: I'm not sure about the stool for the clothes-line. She's not one to hang out her wash.

NAPOLÉON: Sooner or later she'll have to wash her sheets. She's going to run out. That's all she's been wearing since she arrived.

LOUISETTE: Are you doing this just to please her?

NAPOLÉON: No, I want her to forgive me. When I left here earlier I know she was uncomfortable. I reacted so badly when I recognized my "declinquent." I'm sure I hurt her feelings.

LOUISETTE: What's a "declinquent?"

NAPOLÉON: A sort of scumbag. I really did a number on her. Emotional blackmail. You know what that is, eh? No screws, no nails, but solid enough to last a lifetime? It was my late wife's favourite pastime. That and jealousy. When she wanted to know something, she'd go to any lengths to find out. I remember one really hot day like today she dressed herself in winter clothes pretending she was sick.

LOUISETTE: Why?

NAPOLÉON: To find out if I was deceiving her with the checkout girl at the hardware.

LOUISETTE: And?

NAPOLÉON: I ended up saying yes. Every time I denied it, she'd make like she was going to faint. She was wearing three cardigans, a hat, gloves...

LOUISETTE: *(Glancing at the plan.)* What's that there?

NAPOLÉON: A pair of swings. I'll make them with some beautiful wood treated with kreosote, and the deck I'll stain. One gallon of stain should cover about four hundred square feet, so I figure that with four gallons...no, five... They sell pints too, so that would mean approximately twenty pints, but that depends on the brand. There's Sico, C.I.L., Golden Painting...

LOUISETTE: Monsieur Napoléon, what are the swings for?

NAPOLÉON: For the grandchildren.

LOUISETTE: She doesn't have any.

NAPOLÉON: Louis will get down to it one of these days.

LOUISETTE: I'd wait a bit before you cut down the tree.

NAPOLÉON: What about you? I haven't met your fiancé yet.

LOUISETTE: There isn't one.

NAPOLÉON: You know, I haven't stopped talking about your mother, but... By Jeez, you look like a goddess in that outfit!

LOUISETTE: Would you care to put some oil on my back?

NAPOLÉON: Heck, I don't know, that's a dangerous proposition. Which bottle would I use?

LOUISETTE: On the shoulders you put Pre-Sun 15, on the upper back some Tropical Blend 8, Ban de Soleil on the lower back, and on the legs some Hawaiian Tropic 12.

NAPOLÉON: So much for the danger. That's 15, 8, and 12...?

(Facing away from LOUISETTE, he makes a mixture from the different creams.)

I've made you a 35! By the time I figured out your recipe, you'd have had a sunburn.

(He applies the cream.)

LOUISETTE: You do that well.

NAPOLÉON: I practised earlier on my truck. Gave her a nice coat of wax, rubbed her all over. Did a great job.

LOUISETTE: You make me laugh, Monsieur Napoléon.

NAPOLÉON: So much the better!

LOUISETTE: Why don't you get changed and come and sunbathe with me?

NAPOLÉON: *(Suddenly uneasy.)* I'm not a big sunbather.

LOUISETTE: You're shy, maybe?

NAPOLÉON: Well, you know, I like to turn on the charm and all that, and I say some pretty outrageous things, but as for going any further... I guess I do it because...it's something to do.

LOUISETTE: I didn't mean to make you uncomfortable. I just thought we might be friends.

NAPOLÉON: A swell-looking girl like you with an old fart like me?

LOUISETTE: You're no old fart.

NAPOLÉON: I've never had a friend your age.

LOUISETTE: I'm sure there's lots we could learn from each other.

NAPOLÉON: We couldn't be...intimate friends.

LOUISETTE: Why not?

NAPOLÉON: What would people say?

LOUISETTE: Not you too? If we let what people say tell us how to behave, we'll spend the rest of our days walking on eggs!

NAPOLÉON: That's very true. I must write that down.

LOUISETTE: What makes life beautiful are its differences!

NAPOLÉON: But that's precisely what makes people talk.

LOUISETTE: So tell yourself, that's because people like to talk about beautiful things!

NAPOLÉON: Can I tempt you to go for a ride in a beautiful truck? With your new friend?

LOUISETTE: You bet! But in a little while, okay? I've got to straighten out someone else on the subject of what people think.

NAPOLÉON: Who's that?

LOUISETTE: Our professional liar!

NAPOLÉON: When should I start on the deck?

LOUISETTE: When I give the word.

NAPOLÉON: See you later...my friend.

LOUISETTE: See you later...buddy.

(She goes.)

NAPOLÉON: It's amazing! I'm going to go and tell all those old farts around the lake that I've got a girl who's younger than me. I can't wait to see the look on their faces! I'm so proud!

(Blackout.)

Scene Two

> *(Mid-afternoon. It is extremely hot. LOUIS in shorts is writing his thank you cards; GISÈLE, who has her natural grey hair now, is wearing a beach robe. She is reading.)*

LOUIS: *(Writing, absent-mindedly.)* Dear Yannick... Dear Yannick... *(He stops suddenly, realizing what's he's doing. He checks the other cards.)* "Dear Yannick," "Dear Yannick," "Dear Yannick"...

GISÈLE: Did you say something, Louis?

LOUIS: No.

GISÈLE: Get me a glass of water, will you?

LOUIS: Sure.

> *(He doesn't move. A long beat.)*

GISÈLE: My glass of water!

LOUIS: I'm going.

> *(He doesn't move. A longer beat.)*

GISÈLE: Louis!

LOUIS: You haven't finished it already?

GISÈLE: You never brought it to me!

LOUIS: It's so hot I can't move. *(Completely passive.)* How can you read in this heat? It would kill me to turn a page. What are you reading?

GISÈLE: *To Live or to Die.*

LOUIS: Is it interesting?

GISÈLE: *(Closing the book.)* No, depressing!

LOUIS: Have you seen Yannick since this morning?

GISÈLE: No. He left.

LOUIS: Really? The treatment's finished?

GISÈLE: Sort of, yes.

LOUIS: I thought he was very nice.

GISÈLE: Me too.

LOUIS: Charming, in fact.

GISÈLE: Me too.

LOUIS: I really found him attractive.

GISÈLE: Me too. But let's not get depressed. He's gone; he's gone!

LOUIS: I've something to tell you. You won't laugh?

GISÈLE: If it's funny.

LOUIS: Forget it.

GISÈLE: Go on, I won't laugh.

LOUIS: Do you remember the time I brought some friends here to the cottage?

GISÈLE: When?

LOUIS: About five years ago. A guy and his girlfriend.

GISÈLE: Oh yeah, the blond kid with the moustache, and the shorts that were so tight on him he was always getting a headache?

LOUIS: Well, I was his girlfriend.

GISÈLE: Louis, it's too hot, and those kinds of jokes don't make me laugh.

LOUIS:	He and I slept together.
GISÈLE:	Well, I wasn't going to let him sleep with the girl.
LOUIS:	I liked him a lot.
GISÈLE:	It's normal to like one's friends.
LOUIS:	I loved him!
GISÈLE:	Liked, loved, what's the difference?
LOUIS:	I kissed him!
GISÈLE:	So? The French do it all the time.
LOUIS:	If we keep talking like this, it's going to get crude! Maman, I'm trying to tell you the big secret of my life!
GISÈLE:	In this heat?
LOUIS:	I know it may be tough for you, it killed Papa. It's probably irresponsible of me. I like men.
GISÈLE:	So do I. When are you going to get me some water?
LOUIS:	That's all you can say?
GISÈLE:	With some ice!
LOUIS:	Maman, I'm homosexual!
GISÈLE:	So? Does that stop you from getting me water?
LOUIS:	I tell you the big secret of my life and that's all you can say?
GISÈLE:	Secret! Secret! What do you take me for, Louis? I'm your mother!
LOUIS:	You knew?
GISÈLE:	Of course I knew! When your little friend with the tight shorts and the headaches turned up with his so-called girlfriend, I thought it was hysterical. You were being so careful!
LOUIS:	You weren't shocked?

GISÈLE: To see you using a woman like that to hide your little game, yes!

LOUIS: It wasn't a woman.

GISÈLE: *(A beat.)* Science is gaining ground.

LOUIS: You knew, and it never bothered you?

GISÈLE: Come here and give me a hug! *(LOUIS goes to his mother and they embrace.)* I'm glad you've finally told me, now we can be more honest with each other. I've got something to tell you too... *(Long pause.)* I need that glass of water, I'm dry as a bone.

LOUIS: Right away. *(At the door.)* Maman, I think I've fallen in love...

GISÈLE: With who, dear?

LOUIS: With Yannick. Isn't that great?

GISÈLE: Quick, get me that water before I pass out!

> *(He goes in. From inside we hear the telephone ring.)*

I hear you laughing, Fred Cloutier—

LOUIS: *(Off.)* Ayoye!

LOUISETTE: *(Off.)* I have to hang up, Aunt Fer... Yes, that's right, Louis's hurt himself again.

> *(LOUISETTE comes out of the cottage clothed from head to foot. She is wearing sunglasses and clutching a wool cardigan.)*

LOUISETTE: *(Shivering.)* I hope you don't mind, I put a log in the stove.

GISÈLE: The stove! You want to kill us?

LOUISETTE: Do you have any warmer sweaters?

GISÈLE: But you're going to die like that!

LOUISETTE: It's one solution.

GISÈLE: Louisette!

LOUISETTE: I'm so cold.

GISÈLE: What's wrong, sweetheart, are you sick?

LOUISETTE: I'm freezing inside!

GISÈLE: Come on now!

LOUISETTE: I'm sick with love, Maman!

GISÈLE: You're in love?

LOUISETTE: You hear the waves slapping on the shore?

GISÈLE: Yes…what's the connection?

LOUISETTE: Bang! Bang! Bang! That's the sound of my heart, beating
               against his total indifference!

GISÈLE: Wait a minute, here. Who are you in love with?

LOUISETTE: He looks at me, but he doesn't even see me.

GISÈLE: He's blind?

LOUISETTE: Everything's so dark, so hopeless.

GISÈLE: Take off your glasses!

LOUISETTE: My eyes are all puffy, I can't stop crying. I can't stop…I
               can't stop…I can't…

GISÈLE: Louisette, talk sense, you've lost me!

LOUISETTE: Yannick's got to go!

GISÈLE: You mean, you too… *(Calling.)* Never mind the water,
               Louis, bring a bottle of wine! *(Returning to
               LOUISETTE.)* But normally you like them older!

LOUISETTE: I've let a youngster into my heart.

GISÈLE: My poor child!

LOUISETTE: Knowing he's all alone really bothers me!

GISÈLE: Alone?

LOUISETTE: If I could be sure someone loved him. You know what a warm heart I've got.

GISÈLE: No.

LOUISETTE: Yes!

GISÈLE: No.

LOUISETTE: I've got a warm heart!

GISÈLE: Nonsense, you've always been selfish.

LOUISETTE: *(Heading towards the lake.)* Goodbye! I'm going to drown myself.

GISÈLE: *(Stopping her.)* Wait! There is someone in Yannick's life.

LOUISETTE: Oh yeah? Who?

GISÈLE: A woman…quite a bit older…

LOUISETTE: An old lady?

GISÈLE: Heavens, no! I mean…not that old.

LOUISETTE: I'd like to meet her.

GISÈLE: It's complicated.

LOUISETTE: It's a secret?

GISÈLE: Just what I was going to say.

LOUISETTE: She doesn't want anyone to know?

GISÈLE: You took the words right out of my mouth.

LOUISETTE: On account of her age?

GISÈLE: You guessed it.

LOUISETTE: That's so dumb!

GISÈLE: Louisette!

LOUISETTE: I'm boiling!

GISÈLE: It's a woman who was married for a long time, a woman who believed love was something that went on forever with one man. One day she discovered her husband was having an affair with another woman. As time went on, she grew this protective shell around her. When her husband died, she vowed never to fall in love again.

LOUISETTE: And Yannick stumbled into her life a few months after her husband's death?

GISÈLE: That's right.

LOUISETTE: And she's afraid that her kids won't approve?

GISÈLE: It's not really that. You can't rely on a twenty-year-old. When he says "I love you," you can't take it seriously.

LOUISETTE: Who told you that?

GISÈLE: The woman who's in love with Yannick. She believes he means it when he says those things, but she's seen life and she knows that kind of love doesn't last. Young people love too easily, they don't understand the pain it can bring... At my age it's different.

LOUISETTE: You mean, at this other woman's age?

GISÈLE: We're almost the same age.

LOUISETTE: But this other woman, does she love Yannick?

GISÈLE: A lot. She loves him a lot.

LOUISETTE: She must be one of those babes who are always trying to make themselves look younger.

GISÈLE: Not at all!

LOUISETTE: I can see her trying on wigs, putting on face packs...

GISÈLE: She's not like that!

LOUISETTE: I know the type. They lie about their age and about everything else.

GISÈLE: You're going too far, Louisette!

LOUISETTE: And this stupid woman's going to spoil what may be her last chance at happiness because she's scared of being hurt?

GISÈLE: Have some respect for...for her!

LOUISETTE: Well if that's the only reason she won't admit she's having an affair with him, she's nothing but a tease! She's playing this little game just to make him suffer. A woman who can't take hold of her own happiness without making a drama of everything, without worrying what people will say, is nothing but a tease and a masochist! She doesn't realize a relationship like that is a gift—it's the meeting of wisdom and youth! Yannick should leave her.

GISÈLE: What?

LOUISETTE: He should forget her.

GISÈLE: Forget me? Never!

LOUISETTE: I beg your pardon?

GISÈLE: I'm going to tell you something, but you must promise not to laugh.

LOUISETTE: If it's funny...

GISÈLE: Never mind.

LOUISETTE: Say it. I won't laugh.

GISÈLE: The woman I've been talking about is me.

LOUISETTE: *(Mischievous.)* I knew that!

GISÈLE: And you just called me a tease?

LOUISETTE: I've been waiting for this for years.

GISÈLE: You realize you just lied to your mother?

LOUISETTE: I owed you one.

GISÈLE: Does this mean your brother's not in love with him either?

LOUISETTE: Don't be too confident. My God, I'm hot. What's it like
                with Yannick?

GISÈLE: It's a bit hard to talk about…

LOUISETTE: I'm so hot!

GISÈLE: Let's just say that with Yannick I've rediscovered a lot of
                things, things I'd forgotten.

LOUISETTE: I'm burning up!

GISÈLE: Crazy, uninhibited things…feelings I didn't know I still
                had…

                (LOUIS comes out of the cottage.)

LOUIS: Your glass of water, madame. Louisette, it's July!

                *(LOUISETTE grabs the water as he's passing it to
                GISÈLE, and drinks it.)*

LOUISETTE: *(Faintly.)* Are you still there, Maman? Oh, what a pretty
                balloon…

LOUIS: It's the sun, Louisette!

LOUISETTE: I think I'm going to faint.

LOUIS: Quick, take off her clothes!

                *(Enter NAPOLÉON, sporting a pair of outrageous
                Bermuda shorts.)*

NAPOLÉON: Madame Gisèle, I have to speak to you right away!

GISÈLE: Help us remove her clothes!

NAPOLÉON: No problem. Leave me the top, I'll take care of the
                bottom.

GISÈLE: Monsieur Napoléon!

NAPOLÉON: Better now?

LOUIS: Give her some breathing space.

LOUISETTE: *(Coming round.)* Napoléon… My beautiful Napoléon!

LOUIS:	No, it's not better.
NAPOLÉON:	Hello, my beauty! *(To the others.)* We're just friends, nothing more. But if you want to think so, we don't mind, do we, Louisette?
LOUISETTE:	I want a smoke.
NAPOLÉON:	*(To GISÈLE.)* I'm looking for your scumbag!
GISÈLE/ LOUIS:	He's gone!
GISÈLE:	And he's not a scumbag!
NAPOLÉON:	Okay, your "declinquent." He's gone off with my truck! A '64 General motors in perfect condition. If he brings it back with one scratch, one little bump, one scrap of paint missing, he'll get the same treatment!
YANNICK:	*(Entering with a bouquet of flowers.)* Relax, Monsieur Bonneau. Go and look in the yard, your truck's there. Here are the keys. *(To LOUISETTE.)* And here are your cigarettes.
LOUISETTE:	Thanks! You're so tactful! *(Lighting up.)* I promise to stop next summer.
LOUIS:	Don't count on me! Those are quite the shorts, Monsieur Napoléon. Didn't we have a picnic on them somewhere?
LOUISETTE:	His Bermudas are gorgeous! They're different, they make people talk!
YANNICK:	*(Handing the flowers to GISÈLE.)* Forgive me?
GISÈLE:	There's nothing to forgive.
NAPOLÉON:	Why not congratulate him too? Holy Jeez, he bugs me!
YANNICK:	You're so beautiful with your hair like that. Like the first day I saw you.
LOUISETTE:	Maman, don't you have something to tell us?
GISÈLE:	As long as you won't laugh.
EVERYONE:	If it's funny...

GISÈLE: Forget it.

EVERYONE: We won't laugh. Go on!

GISÈLE: Yannick and I...we...we've been in love for two months.

LOUISETTE: That wasn't so hard?

LOUIS: Speak for yourself, Louisette! Do you realize how old he is?

GISÈLE: What's wrong with that? Your father was no older when I first met him. *(To YANNICK.)* I love you!

NAPOLÉON: Jesus, Mary and Joseph!

YANNICK: Again!

NAPOLÉON: Jesus, Mary and Joseph!

YANNICK: Not you. Her!

GISÈLE: I love you, Puss!

YANNICK: I love you too, Petunia!

GISÈLE: My handsome Puss!

YANNICK: My precious Pooh!

LOUIS: Go right ahead, enjoy yourselves! What about me?

                 (YANNICK takes a flower from GISÈLE's bouquet and gives it to LOUIS.)

YANNICK: I'm sorry about last night. *(He kisses him.)* That's the first one, and the last!

NAPOLÉON: Holy Jeez!

                 (We hear the horn from a truck.)

YANNICK: I almost forgot. Do you have fifty bucks?

GISÈLE: What for?

YANNICK: To pay the guy with the tow truck.

GISÈLE: What tow truck?

YANNICK: I missed a curve with Napoléon's truck.

NAPOLÉON: Listen, buddy, do you know what a steering wheel's for?

YANNICK: If you're going to buy vehicles just 'cause they look good! Hell, you can't rely on what you steal these days!

NAPOLÉON: How'd'ya like to end up in a vacuum cleaner bag?

LOUIS: I'll look after the tow truck. *(He exits.)*

LOUISETTE: There's something important we still have to do.

(LOUISETTE goes into the cottage, followed by NAPOLÉON.)

GISÈLE: You don't need a rehabilitation programme, you need driving lessons! Your flowers are lovely. Did you pay for them?

YANNICK: Hey! *(A beat.)* I know you're afraid I'll leave, that I'll find you too old someday, but don't forget, I'm going to get older too. It's the only thing we all have in common in this world, getting older.

GISÈLE: No more lies, I promise.

YANNICK: Me neither.

GISÈLE: You've never lied to me.

YANNICK: The flowers? I didn't pay for them.

GISÈLE: And the cigarettes?

YANNICK: Hey...!

GISÈLE: You wait! Some things are going to change!

(LOUISETTE and NAPOLÉON come out of the cottage with the funeral urn. LOUIS returns.)

We were doing so nicely, we were starting to be happy, but no... Well, Fred Cloutier, it's time to get even!

LOUISETTE: To calm us all down tonight, we're going to start building the new deck. Napoléon's drawn this wonderful plan.

NAPOLÉON: And guess what, Yannick? You're going to be pounding a lot of nails!

GISÈLE: So much for our romantic weekend!

LOUISETTE: Louis, wipe that smirk off your face. Ever since you paid for the tow truck, you've been grinning like an idiot.

LOUIS: I'm afraid I can't help you with the deck tonight. I've got a date. A towing lesson.

NAPOLÉON: Jesus, Mary and Joseph!

YANNICK: *(Pointing to the urn.)* What's in there?

GISÈLE: My husband. He deceived me, and look where that got him. Consider yourself warned!

LOUISETTE: Time to take care of Papa!

NAPOLÉON: We can take my boat. Fourteen feet of aluminum! It's an Atalqua: forty horsepower, stainless steel propellor... Aren't you just dying to know how much gas it takes?

EVERYONE: No!

YANNICK: Hey, wouldn't you like me to drive?

EVERYONE: No!

YANNICK: Just kidding!

LOUISETTE: Come on, folks, time to head out! The leeches are waiting.

GISÈLE: Poor leeches!

(The End.)